DARK TESTAMENT

AND
OTHER
POEMS

OTHER BOOKS BY PAULI MURRAY

Song in a Weary Throat

Proud Shoes

States' Laws on Race and Color

The Constitution and Government of Ghana

(coauthor with Leslie Rubin)

Human Rights U.S.A.: 1948–1966

DARK TESTAMENT

AND
OTHER
POEMS

PAULI MURRAY

WITH A NEW INTRODUCTION BY ELIZABETH ALEXANDER

LIVERIGHT PUBLISHING CORPORATION
A Division of W. W. Norton & Company
Independent Publishers Since 1923
New York | London

For information about special discounts for bulk purchases, please contact
W. W. Norton Special Sales at specialsales@wwnorton.com or 800-233-4830

Manufacturing by Versa Press
Book design by Chris Welch
Production manager: Beth Steidle

ISBN 978-1-63149-483-3

Liveright Publishing Corporation, 500 Fifth Avenue, New York, N.Y. 10110
www.wwnorton.com

W. W. Norton & Company Ltd., 15 Carlisle Street, London W1D 3BS

1 2 3 4 5 6 7 8 9 0

CONTENTS

III

"I . . . am not contain'd between my hat and my boots."

IV

NO GREENER SPRING

INTRODUCTION

One life, two lives, three lives, more: Pauli Murray made an indelible mark on American history in multiple modes rarely found in one career. Legal crusader and theorist; activist; educator, first ordained black female Episcopal priest; cofounder of a national women's rights organization. Murray put mind, spirit, and body on the line for justice. Why—or how—did such a variously accomplished person also choose to seriously pursue writing poetry as a constant throughout her life? What does the practice of poetry accomplish and allow that the other areas of Murray's brilliance could not?

I hesitate to say "brilliance" because Pauli Murray's accomplishments were always in service to principles and people, not for the sake of a traditional supernova self or "great person" of history. But surely Murray was a genius, in service of justice. Murray authored what Thurgood Marshall called "the bible" of the civil rights movement, her 1950 book *States' Law on Race and Color.* She continually made a way out of no way, finding spaces in which to learn and excel and share. Murray was an intersectional analyst on race, gender, and class before those who would develop the theory and the phrase were born. Civil disobedience was one of her tools; she was arrested for refusing to sit in the back of the bus years before Rosa Parks and the subsequent Montgomery bus boycott. Murray was an influential academic cofounder of the National Organization of Women. She coined the phrase "Jane Crow," which wrote gender into the racial thinking and analysis that drove the civil rights movement. And she moved beyond her intellectual and activist accomplishments to the spiritual life when she studied to become an Episcopal priest, breaking new ground to gather her community in vision.

Why and how poetry? Murray faced and explored the interior space between certainty and uncertainty, and poetry allowed her to be in those spaces without contradiction. The law seems to promise certainty, the pleasure and reward of a set of powerful tools, and that is one way to go about making change. But I think Murray was interested in self simultaneously in and outside of gender constraints. Poetry was where she could imagine herself into other identities and experiences. In deeply imagined persona poems, Murray brought her readers into the experience of lynching and other forms of racial violence. She illuminated the courage of young people in the face of such demonic opposition and seemingly impassable straits. Sometimes in doing the work of political struggle we do not pause long enough in the human stories themselves. Murray used poetry as a tool to slow down and experience, deeply, what it means to be among the most vulnerable and the most resilient.

Murray's experience of gender was not fixed by social norms, and her admission and embrace of her gender fluidity was highly unusual in her times. How she lived in gender surfaces the deepest human questions: Who am I? What do I desire? How am I oriented? Where is my sun, my north star? In her poetry we see the Pauli Murray who experienced curiosity without certainty, beyond the societal definitions. For a person so uncannily accomplished, with such tremendous capacity to improve the conditions of others, her poems are an argument for the need for an introspective and expressive self-practice in order to best do the work of public-facing justice advocacy.

Murray was familiar with disturbances of the self in the mind. Her father died in the Hospital for the Negro Insane of Maryland (Crownsville) when she was thirteen years old, beaten to death by a white guard. She herself was hospitalized at Bellevue following a romantic crisis, and perhaps also other struggles. It seemed she understood poetry as a space for exploration and self knowing, for crystallizing perception and disturbance into form, and thus, for a moment, subduing the roiling seas. I mention this to say that the example of her complex, self-aware life that is always seeking to love and connect is a prescient beacon, and why she endures today and seems so modern is that that richness is in fact in all of us, whether or not we achieve renown for our deeds.

Murray explored uncertainty in her poetry and thus brought her unalloyed self to her public work, her teaching and activism. Poetry also allowed her to distill some of the justice principles she lived by and thought for. Some of these poems are like anthems, flags for the work she did and maps of the interior self who did this work.

The poem "Prophecy" is one example:

I sing of a new American
Separate from all others,
Yet enlarged and diminished by all others.
I am the child of kings and serfs, freeman and slaves,
Having neither superiors nor inferiors,
Progeny of all colors, all cultures, all systems, all beliefs.
I have been enslaved, yet my spirit is unbound.
I have been cast aside, but I sparkle in the darkness.
I have been slain but live on in the rivers of history.
I seek no conquest, no wealth, no power, no revenge;
I seek only discovery
Of the illimitable heights and depths of my own being.

For some, the great deed eclipses the interior life. Some live without love and intimacy but Pauli Murray was not one of them. It is in her poetry that we see the full dimension, and these words remind us that the mightiest warrior can suffer in love and be positively motivated by love. Her poems suggest that perhaps freedom also must contain a component of love, and that the clearest beacon of intellect could experience confusion in heart and soul space.

Murray writes in the poem "Love's More Enduring Uses,"

But love, alas, holds me captive here,
Consigned to sacrificial flame, to burn

And find no heart's surcease until
Its more enduring uses I may learn.

Murray lived a life fueled by duty, mission, justice, rescue, learning, sharing knowledge, fighting the power. But also in these poems, a life characterized by deep love, longing, love lost. Murray's poems show us the fullness of the person "superb in love and logic," to quote Robert Hayden's poem "Frederick Douglass." Love and logic, twinned and indivisible.

With these poems, we have the complete Pauli Murray.

—*Elizabeth Alexander*

To the many friends who have made this book possible
and to the memory of Eleanor Roosevelt

Friends and countrymen!

I speak for my race and my people—

The human race and just people.

DARK TESTAMENT

(In Memory of Stephen Vincent Benét)

1

Freedom is a dream
Haunting as amber wine
Or worlds remembered out of time.
Not Eden's gate, but freedom
Lures us down a trail of skulls
Where men forever crush the dreamers—
Never the dream.

I was an Israelite walking a sea bottom,
I was a Negro slave following the North Star,
I was an immigrant huddled in ship's belly,
I was a Mormon searching for a temple,
I was a refugee clogging roads to nowhere—
Always the dream was the same—
Always the dream was freedom.

2

America was a new dream and a new world for dreaming.
America was the vast sleeping Gulliver of the globe.
America was the dream of freedom.
But the dream was lost when campfires grew,
The Bible twisted as white men threw
The Redskins back to mountain pass,
The senses dulled with whiskey flask,
The arrow broken by searing lead.
"Better to die," the Red Man said.

The white slave ran away too soon,
Followed the path of dying moon—
A face forgotten in frontier shack
Where none asked questions, few turned back,
Here was a place where a man could stand
Holding free earth in scrawny hand.
Here was a world where freedom was won
By the hand on an axe, the hand on a gun.

3

Free earth hungered for free men but
Free men soon hungered for gold.
Planters bargained with traders,
        traders bargained with slavers,
Slavers turned toward Africa.
The dream was lost in the quest for gold.

The men of Africa were stalwart men,
Tough as hickory deep in their primal forests,
Their skins the color of tree-bark—
Ebony, bamboo, cocoanut, mango—
Their hair was thick with jungle,
Their eyes were dark as star-fed night.
They were sly and cunning, fearless and cool,
They knew the cry of every forest bird and beast.

Smelters of iron, carvers of wood and ivory,
Weavers and potters of intricate design,
Followers of the honeybird to the honeytree,
Hunters of antelope, lion and elephant,
Some were gentle tribes and some were fiercely brave,
Warriors of the poisoned spear
Testing their strength in battle man for man.
And when they killed the foe, they ate his heart
To make themselves invincible.

Story-tellers all, refusing to be hurried,
Who nightly by the village fires
Recalled their tribal history,
Evoked ancestral heroes,
Imbued their young with pride.
And every task no matter what its import
Signalled a joyous song and tribal dance.

4

O black warrior,
Hurl a dark spear of song
Borne on a night-wind
Piercing the sorrow-haunted darkness—
Perpetual cycle of grief,
Cruel legacy of endless betrayal,
Frenzied anger beating against
Impenetrable walls of silence!

Ours is no bedtime story children beg to hear,
No heroes rode down the night to warn our
        sleeping villages.
Ours is a tale of blood streaking the Atlantic—
        From Africa to Barbados
        From Haiti to Massachusetts,
        From Rhode Island to Virginia,
        From the red clay of Georgia
        To requiem in Memphis,
        From swampy graves in Mississippi
        To the morgues of Detroit.

Ours is a tale of charred and blackened fruit,
Aborted harvest dropped from blazing bough,
A tale of eagles exiled from the nest,
Brooding and hovering on the edge of sky—
A somber shadow on this native earth,
Yet no faint tremor of her breast
Eludes the circle of our hungered eye.

5

Black men were safe when tom-toms slumbered
'Til traders came with beads and rum,
Bartered and bribed on their slaver's quest,
Killed the watcher, silenced the drum.

Villages screamed in headless horror,
Villages blazed with fiery eye,
Trapped lions roared no greater terror
Than man pinned back on burning sky.
With one great throat the forests thundered,
With one vast body their creatures fled
But man the hunter was now the hunted
Bleeding fresh trails of dying and dead.

Tethered beneath a slave-ship's girth,
The hours throbbed with dying and birth,
Foaming and champing in slime and dung,
Rumbling curses in a jungle tongue,
Torturous writhing of limbs that burst,
Whimpering children choked with thirst,
Vomiting milk from curdled breast,
Rat's teeth sinking in suckling's chest,
Slave ships plunging through westing waves,
Grinding proud men to cringing slaves.

"Oh, running slaves is a risky trade
When you cross the path of Gov'ment sail,
They'll smell you five miles down the wind
For a slaver stinks like a rotting whale.
And when they spy you, dump your cargo,
Shove the first black over the rail . . ."

He twists, he spins, he claws at the sun,
He plummets down, dark dagger in the flood,
He sucks in the others one by one
And the foam track crimsons with their blood
As glistening shark fins flash among
The black heads bobbing on the wave,
The slave ship flees and freedom is won
In churning torrent, in fathomless grave.

6

We have not forgotten the market square—
Malignant commerce in our flesh—
Huddled like desolate sheep—
Tumult of boisterous haggling—
We waited the dreadful moment of dispersal.
One by one we climbed the auction block—
Naked in an alien land—

Driven by whip's relentless tongue
To dance and caper in the sun,
Ripple the muscles from shoulders to hips,
To show the teeth and bulge the biceps,
To feel the shame of a girl whose breasts
Are bared to squeeze of a breeder's fists.

Sold! Resold with the same coin
Our unrewarded sweat had borne.
Endless tearing—man wrested from woman
Warm and brown as sunflower heart,
Plucked up, thrust down in untamed earth,
Uprooted, dispersed again—she was too brief a wife.
She sits in frozen grief
And stares with mindless eyes
At fatherless children crying in the night.

7

Trade a king's freedom for a barrel of molasses,
Trade a queen's freedom for a red bandanna,
Or Cherokee-mulattoes in North Carolina,
Or a Creole mistress in Louisiana.
Sell a man's brain for a handful of greenbacks,
Mark him up in Congress—he's three-fifths human,
Mark him down in the record with mules and mortgage,
Sell him long! Sell him short! Cotton's a-boomin'.
Take a black's manhood, give a white God,
Send him 'way down in the dismal woods
Where a black man's tears will not embarrass
A white man's juleps and lofty moods.

A black man down on his knees in the swamp-grass
Sent his prayer straight to the white God's throne,
Built him a faith, built a bridge to this God
And God gave him hope and the power of song.

8

Hope is a crushed stalk
Between clenched fingers.
Hope is a bird's wing
Broken by a stone.
Hope is a word in a tuneless ditty—
A word whispered with the wind,
A dream of forty acres and a mule,
A cabin of one's own and a moment to rest,
A name and place for one's children
And children's children at last . . .
Hope is a song in a weary throat.

> *Give me a song of hope*
> *And a world where I can sing it.*
> *Give me a song of faith*
> *And a people to believe in it.*
> *Give me a song of kindliness*
> *And a country where I can live it.*
> *Give me a song of hope and love*
> *And a brown girl's heart to hear it.*

9

Pity the poor who hate—
Wild brood of earth's lean seasons—
Pity the poor, the land-robbed whites,
Driven by planters to marshy back-lands,
Driven by fevers, pellagra and hookworm,
Driven to hate niggers warm in their cabins,
The nigger fed on scraps from the Big House,
The nigger's hands on a fine tall coach-whip,
The half-white nigger in a rich man's kitchen.

Give 'em a chance they'd burn that nigger,
Burn 'im on a tree in the swamp-lands,
Teach 'im not to eat while white men hungered,
Teach 'im that even God is white
And had no time for niggers' praying,
Teach 'im that the devil is black
And niggers were the sons of evil.

> *Pity slave and serf in their misery,*
> *Bound by common fate to common destiny.*

10

The drivers are dead now
But the drivers have sons.
The slaves are dead too
But the slaves have sons,
And when sons of drivers meet sons of slaves
The hate, the old hate, keeps grinding on.
Traders still trade in double-talk
Though they've swapped the selling-block
For ghetto and gun!

> *This is our portion, this is our testament,*
> *This is America, dual-brained creature,*
> *One hand thrusting us out to the stars,*
> *One hand shoving us down in the gutter.*

Pile up the records, sing of pioneers,
Point to images chipped from mountain-heart,
Swagger through history with glib-tongued traditions,
Say of your grass roots, "We are a hard-ribbed people,
One nation indivisible with liberty and justice for all."

> *Put it all down in a time capsule,*
> *Bury it deep in the soil of Virginia,*
> *Bury slave-song with the Constitution,*
> *Bury it in that vineyard of planters*
> *And poll-taxers, sharecroppers and Presidents.*
> *In coffin and outhouse all men are equal,*
> *And the same red earth is fed*
> *By the white bones of Tom Jefferson*
> *And the white bones of Nat Turner.*

11

Tear it out of the history books!
Bury it in conspiracies of silence!
Fight many wars to suppress it!
But it is written in our faces
Twenty million times over!

> *It sings in our blood,*
> *It cries from the housetops,*
> *It mourns with the wind in the forests,*
> *When dogs howl and will not be comforted,*
> *When newborn lambs bleat in the snowdrifts,*
> *And dead leaves rattle in the graveyards.*
> *And we'll shout it from the mountains,*
> *We'll tell it in the valleys,*
> *We'll talk it in miner's shack,*
> *We'll sing it at the work bench,*
> *We'll whisper it over back fences,*
> *We'll speak it in the kitchen,*
> *We'll state it at the White House,*
> *We'll tell it everywhere to all who will listen—*

We will lay siege, let thunder serve our claim,
For it must be told, endlessly told, and you
        must hear it.
Listen, white brothers, hear the dirge of history,
And hold out your hand—hold out your hand.

12

Of us who darkly stand
Bared to the spittle of every curse,
Nor left the dignity of beasts,
Let none say, "Those were not men
But cowards all, with eyes dull-lidded as a frog's.
They labored long but not from love,
They strove from blind perpetual fear."

Better our seed rot on the ground
And our hearts burn to ash
Than the years be empty of our imprint.
We have no other dream, no land but this;
With slow deliberate hands these years
Have set her image on our brows.
We are her seed, have borne a fruit
Native and pure as unblemished cotton.

> *Then let the dream linger on.*
> *Let it be the test of nations,*
> *Let it be the quest of all our days,*
> *The fevered pounding of our blood,*
> *The measure of our souls—*
> *That none shall rest in any land*

And none return to dreamless sleep,
No heart be quieted, no tongue be stilled
Until the final man may stand in any place
And thrust his shoulders to the sky,
Friend and brother to every other man.

II

I am the American heartbreak—

—LANGSTON HUGHES

Color Trouble

If you dislike me just because
My face has more of sun than yours,
Then, when you see me, turn and run
But do not try to bar the sun.

February 1938

To the Oppressors

Now you are strong
And we are but grapes aching with ripeness.
Crush us!
Squeeze from us all the brave life
Contained in these full skins.
But ours is a subtle strength
Potent with centuries of yearning,
Of being kegged and shut away
In dark forgotten places.

We shall endure
To steal your senses
In that lonely twilight
Of your winter's grief.

Mulatto's Dilemma

I curse the summer sun
That burned me thus to fateful recognition.
Should such a thought strike terror to my frame
More than another? I am the strongest of this lot
And fit to do the work of two. Were I but paler
By a single tone they would not see me tremble;
Or if in shackles here, they'd buy my strength
And let another starve—but being free,
(If being dark is freedom),—they stare
At me; they note the curl below my hat;
They trace the darker line below my chin.

Oh God! My face has slipped them but my soul
Cries with the fear of brownness before a bar
Where brown's already judged by sight. Can I
Endure the killing weight of time it takes them
To be sure?

        If I could lay my quivering brain
Before them, they'd see a brain is but a brain
And know that brown men think and feel, are hurt
And broken even as they.

            Oh, for the pride
Of blackness! To stand unmasked before them,
Nor moved by inquisition. Accepted or refused—
Not crucified.

Mr. Roosevelt Regrets

(Detroit Riot, 1943)

Upon reading PM newspaper's account of Mr. Roosevelt's statement on the recent race clashes: *"I share your feeling that the recent outbreaks of violence in widely spread parts of the country endanger our national unity and comfort our enemies. I am sure that every true American regrets this."*

What'd you get, black boy,
When they knocked you down in the
    gutter,
And they kicked your teeth out,
And they broke your skull with clubs
And they bashed your stomach in?
What'd you get when the police shot
    you in the back,
And they chained you to the beds
While they wiped the blood off?
What'd you get when you cried out to
    the Top Man?
When you called on the man next to
    God, so you thought,
And you asked him to speak out to save
    you?
What'd the Top Man say, black boy?
"Mr. Roosevelt regrets . . . ."

27

Harlem Riot, 1943

Not by hammering the furious word,
Nor bread stamped in the streets,
Nor milk emptied in gutter,
Shall we gain the gates of the city.

But I am a prophet without eyes to see;
I do not know how we shall gain the gates
        of the city.

August, 1943

The Passing of F.D.R.

"PRESIDENT ROOSEVELT IS DEAD"
New York Times, dateline April 12, 1945

A lone man stood on the glory road,
Peered through the shadows,
Made sure he was alone—at last,
Then drank a new-found solitude,
Drank long and deep of the vast
Breath of lilacs and honeysuckle.

He stumbled a pace,
Groped about in the April twilight
As one who feels his legs beneath him
For the first time,
Tests them on solid earth
And finds them worthy of a good sprint.

The man laughed, a golden laughter,
Rich and deep as a Georgia sunset,
Lifted a foot and kicked a pebble,
Shouted and sang, danced up and down,
As do all free things
Finding themselves free.

His shoulders spread like an eagle's wing
Freed from some killing weight, and so
Putting one foot down before the other
He strode with a whistling gait.

And then his face, miracle of light,
Gay and soft as a child's
Retrieving a beloved toy,
Turned toward the going sun,
Turned to the hills and the long road upward.

It is such a common thing to see
A man walking a road in Georgia twilight,
But if you had been watching
Or held your ear to the ground long enough,
You would have known this man
Walked as few had done before him.

There was the sound of marching in his step—
A world marching,
There was the patter of children's feet,
There was earth music, a million-voiced hymn,
And a great prayer thrust up in many tongues,
A small dog's barking, a small lad's tears,
And the silence of a world aged with grief.

Oh, bare your breast to the grindstone, brothers,
Let the heart's filings fill this crack in time,
For a lone man walks on the glory road,
Waits for the final gun,
The last exploding cannon,
When a man can walk in Georgia twilight,
Shouting as all free things do
Finding themselves free.

Collect for Poplarville

(ADAPTED FROM *THE BOOK OF COMMON PRAYER*)

Lighten our darkness, we beseech thee, O Lord;
    Teach us no longer to dread
        hounds yelping in the distance,
        the footfall at the door,
        the rifle butt on the window pane.

And by thy great mercy defend us from all perils
    and dangers of this night;
        Give us fearlessness to face
            the bomb thrown from the darkness,
            the gloved hand on the pistol,
            the savage intention.
        Give us courage to stand firm against
            our tormentors without rancor—
        Teach us that most difficult of tasks—
            to pray for them,
            to follow, not burn, thy cross!

New York, May 1959

For Mack C. Parker

(VICTIM OF LYNCHING IN MISSISSIPPI, 1959)

In the hour of death,
In the day of judgment,
  Good Lord, deliver us!

The Book of Common Prayer

The cornered and trapped,
The bludgeoned and crushed,
The hideously slain,
Freed from the dreaded waiting,
The tortured body's pain,
On death's far shore cast mangled shrouds
To clothe the damned whose fear
Decreed a poisoned harvest,
Garnered a bitter grain.
For these who wear the cloak of shame
Must eat the bread of gall,
Each vainly rubbing the 'cursed spot
Which brands him Cain.

April 1959

Ruth

Brown girl chanting Te Deums on Sunday
Rust-colored peasant with strength of granite,
Bronze girl welding ship hulls on Monday,
Let nothing smirch you, let no one crush you.

Queen of ghetto, sturdy hill-climber,
Walk with the lilt of ballet dancer,
Walk like a strong down-East wind blowing,
Walk with the majesty of the First Woman.

Gallant challenger, millioned-hope bearer,
The stars are your beacons, earth your inheritance,
Meet blaze and cannon with your own heart's passion,
Surrender to none the fire of your soul.

Psalm of Deliverance

(To the Negro School Children of the
American South in the Year 1959)

1

Children of courage, we great you!
Gentle warriors, we salute you!

Youthful veterans of upheaval,
Victims of mindless resistance,

We, the wounded and dead of former campaigns,
Unknown, unheralded, unribboned,

The nameless millions, native and migrant,
We are legion and we support you!

From restless graves in swamps and bayous,
From slave ships, slave pens, chain gangs and prisons,

From ruined churches and blazing lynch-trees,
From gas chambers and mass crematoriums,

From foxholes, ghettoes, detention camps,
From lonely outposts of exclusion,

We hear your marching feet and rise,
Silently we walk beside you!

> *We have returned from a place beyond hope;*
> *We have returned from wastelands of despair;*
> *We have come to reclaim our heritage;*
> *We have come to redeem our honor!*

2

They padlocked school doors, closed the gates to knowledge,
Trafficked in calumny, spread evil rumors,

Like timber wolves stalking stray sheep,
Hunted us down, drove us from our homes, slew us.

Frenzied, they turned on their own God,
Dynamited His churches and temples!

Stampeded like fire-crazed wild herds;
Silenced voices of reason; trampled one another.

Frantic, they strove by harsh enactments,
Crafty delays, witless improvisations

To turn back our tides of inexorable insistence,
Hinder the oncoming flood of our destiny.

Victims of self-delusion,
Misread our calmness as acquiescence.

But we are veterans of countless battles,
Steeled in crucibles of unequal contests,

Tempered by struggle, disciplined by sorrow
To granite endurance; now we are resolute!

We have remembered what they have forgotten,
Learning our lesson well, forgetting nothing—

>*We have returned from a place beyond hope;*
>*We have returned from wastelands of despair;*
>*We have come to reclaim our heritage;*
>*We have come to redeem our honor!*

3

We were the vanquished, the self-exiled;
Renounced our inheritance, land of our fathers;

We were the wanderers; journeyed to cities,
Searching and seeking, seeking and searching;

Plunged into entrails of ghettoes,
Submerged in garbage of slumlands;

Toiled by day, learned by night,
Won degrees from great universities—

Found them worthless souvenirs of effort
Yellowing in a drawer or battered suitcase,

Valued less than leavings of cigarettes
Scooped from gutters and hoarded in cans!

Flotsam in tenements, watchers at knotholes,
Barred from the contest, rusting from disuse;

Condemned to idleness; frozen to bottom rung;
Battling cockroaches in cheap rooming houses;

Passed over in hiring halls—*"They don't hire colored!"*
"No job available—you're overqualified!"

"Help Wanted—Whites only need apply!"
"Careers for college-trained—Whites only!"

"Travel opportunities—Colored excluded!"
"Double feature tonight—Negroes upstairs!"

We pawned our clothes, class pins and watches;
Tried to buy jobs as unskilled laborers. No go!

We, too, have known ultimate surrender,
Hauled down our tattered pride, made the long march—

The last cent was borrowed, nothing left to pawn,
The hominy grits gave out, the cigarette butts were gone.

The rent was overdue, the salt-and-water
No longer eased our hunger pains.

We have gone, not without shame,
Sneaking like thieves in the night, concealing our hurt,

To the office of Emergency Home Relief!
Waited our turn to nibble at Public Assistance!

Stripped down until we were naked,
Our secrets exposed; our private embarrassments

All written down in a public record—
Exchanged our pride for a Case Number—

The city's poor, society's backwash,
Painfully learning the rules of the destitute.

We have remembered what many have forgotten—
Out of those bitter days comes an epitaph—

> *Name:* Henry Jones (or James Smith or Lucy Brown)
> *Place of Birth:* U.S.A.—Any town or hamlet south of
> Washington, D.C.
> *Age:* Twenty-three.
> *Education:* A.B., Graduate of City College, Class of '33
> *Occupation:* Unemployed.
> *Race:* Negro (circled as practically unemployable)
> *Residence:* Formerly YMCA, but vague as to last six months.
> Probably sleeps in subway or park.
> *Skills:* Majored in Social Science and History. No professional
> experience; has held part-time jobs as clerical worker,
> handyman, dishwasher, elevator operator,
> porter, janitor.

Reason for leaving last job: Reduction in personnel
(last hired, first fired).
Disposition: Certified to W.P.A. at $23.86 per week, where in
time he will be identified as a *boondoggler!* Case
closed in Home Relief Files with the following
notation:
"In his twenty-fourth year, his youth died!"

We have remembered, and remembering,
We rise from the shadows and stand beside you!

We have returned from a place beyond hope;
We have returned from wastelands of despair;
We have come to reclaim our heritage;
We have come to redeem our honor!

MacDowell Colony, May 1959

I . . . am not contain'd
between my hat and my boots.

—*Walt Whitman*

Youth to Age

Aged one and wise,
Were you twenty-two again
Would you risk all for fame?
Conform?
Or go your way alone?

But how can you reply, being seventy-two?
Your path is fogged with memories
As mine with fears.

Youth, 1933

I

I sing of Youth, imperious, inglorious;
Dissatisfied, unslaked, untaught, unkempt Youth.
Youth who admits neither God nor country,
Youth proud and eager—proud of its broken heads,
Eager to martyr itself for any and all Causes.

II

Youth, bloody with flags; hot with protests;
Youth who would wage war, decrying War;
Armed with pistols, razors, knives,
Armed with gin-bottles and machine guns,
Armed with tin cans and broom handles,
Armed with rotten eggs and tomatoes,
Armed with red banners, placards and worthless diplomas.

Youth perched on soap-boxes, platforms and ladders,
Preaching to any who will stop to listen;
Giving out hand-bills, pamphlets and tickets—
"The true information, the one authentic
Story of this case or that case,—
The trouble with the world is—you'll find it right here!
Read it, Comrade, and join the Movement!"

III

Youth who boasts of its strong personality,
Youth who is certain of its individuality,—
Yet dares not walk alone, stand alone, think alone;
But cries, "Follow the Leader! Follow the Leader!
Follow the Leader to Washington! To London! To Berlin!
We've got to see the President! The Premier! The Chancellor!
We'll get what the Administration has failed to get!
We've so much to offer—such Faith and such Vision,—
Damn the historians! Damn the experienced!
We've nothing to lose!"

IV

Fighting, bleeding, falling, dying,—
Dying for the Movement—
"Down with the Capitalists! The bourgeois! the lynchers!
Down with Politics! Ethics! Religion!
Down with everything but the Youth Movement!—
Never mind what it means—on with the Movement!"

V

Youth apathetic, youth energetic,
Breeding children before they are striplings,
Destroying Life before they've begun Life.
Peace conferences ending in bedlam and riot,
Race meetings boiling the pot of Race Hatred—
Communist, Socialist, Negro and Jew—
Sore spots of Nations.

VI

On they go, this Youth the world over,
Headed for Chaos with wrangling and snarling,
Bursting all bonds, junking all ideals,
Shouting in chorus, "We protest! We demand!"

Having one weapon, they wield it unsparingly—
Youth—hot-headedness, energy, passion.
"Make way, you slackers, money-hounds, Party guns!
We are your Leaders, trust or outlaw us,—
We are the Youth of the World's New Deal!"

New York, 1933

The Newer Cry

I am weary, O God, of dark lamentations,
Of angry voices and sullen faces,
Of empty hands stretched heavenward
Pleading for mercy and justice.

We are not dumb driven beasts—
We are men!
Our hands have been taught
To work and to fight.

We have known bondage,
We have known hunger and need,
We have known pain and humiliation;
But man is slave only to himself,
And pain is but the door to deeper Understanding.

Let us laugh—not in deceit,
Not in childish pleasure—but out of gladness,—
Joy in our youth, pride in our strength.

Let us view all men with calm untroubled eyes,
But never grow smug in our own self-righteousness;
Let us give pity where pity is due, but scorn it
From our inferiors.
Let us grow strong, but never in our strength
Forget the weaker brother.

Let us fight—but only when we must fight!

Let us work—for therein lies our salvation;
Let us conquer the soil—for therein lies our sustenance;
Let us conquer the soul—for therein lies our power;
Let us march!—in steady unbroken beat—
For therein lies our progress.

Let us never cease to laugh, to live, to love and to grow.

New York, 1933

Hate

Heaven hates with cosmic ire,
The star point breaks,
The earth's core cracks
And fire-tongued mountains
Consume a sleeping valley.

But when man hates
His clumsy hands drip human blood,
And where, in some quiet land
White goats danced on a hillside
Or children gathered flowers,
A thousand puny skulls
Give feast to flies and maggots.

Quarrel

Two ants at bay
on the curved stem of an apple
are insufficient cause
to fell the tree.

November 1937

To Poets Who Have Rebelled

Decry, as you must, this frenzied world,
Thunder your wrath around the curve of earth
That flesh must cry of hunger, breeding flesh
To feed the mouth of flame. Decry the lean
Of lips to lips unclean, the sodden streets
And hunger-twisted children, and all the shame
And ugliness of greed and hate.

Hail, as you must, a tractored and turbined world
To lift the pressing earth from weary backs
And let men turn face outward to the sky
Filling their horny hands with golden air;

But let your throats ache double
With the cry of beauty here and now,
When the hand clings to the root
And the forearm guides the plow,
And the heart marks common pulse
With time beating through the sky.

Hail, if you must, your barricades,
Your enemy thwarted, and you and they
Lying in piles of carrion-food
Where once were laughing voices;

But take not from man's eyes
The flash of blade on wet grass
Nor from his ears the swish of the sickle.

Whatever is good
Does not always cry with the color of banners
Or shout with the thunder of drums,
Or rush on wings of cannon—
It sometimes descends, slowly, as night
Or grows in silence as the lifting dawn.

Whatever is good is not more
Than the world-shaking event
Of planting a rose,
Or plucking a truant weed,
Or watching a chimney-swallow after rain
Patiently restoring its nest.

Whatever is good lies at the core
Of the clean brown soil,
When a man smelling of earthiness
Looks at the sun through mist
And says to himself,
"Tomorrow brings rain for the young corn,
Tomorrow the apple trees will blossom;
That is good."

Let it suffice for a moment
If a man can stand in the wind
Seeing gold in the wheat-fields,
Hearing a chorus of corn-leaves
And whisper, "Life is good."

Let it be enough for the moment
If he can race with a cloud to a hilltop,
And throwing himself on a grass-mound
Lay his lips to warm earth.

New York, February 1938

Tongues

It is quite possible, I think,
That tongues, not money,
Are taproots of evil.
If men were mutes and could not babble
There'd be less need for conferences,
Caucuses, rallies, meetings, speeches—
The tongue dragging the body around.

New York, 1939

The Song of the Highway

I am the Highway,
Long, white, winding Highway,
Binding coast to coast
And people to people;
I am the spine of the earth.

Over the hills I glide
And then, come swooping down
To some deserted spot.
Over river and lake I stride—
Through farm and field, and town,
Through desert sands, white-hot.

I laugh when the brooklets laugh,
And weep with wayside trees
So bent—so broken by the wind.
Sometimes the birds and flowers
Fill my path with song and bloom;
Sometimes a fragrant breeze
Leaves me drenched with faint perfume.

I hear the sounds of earth—
The low of cattle on the plains,
Clatter of hoof, sound of horn,
Rustling fields of rye,
Of wheat, of tassled corn;
Sweet sounds, so dear—
As through the year
Life marches on.

I am old—sad things I know,
Ache of road-worn travelers,
Lonely hours; the tragedy of pioneers
Who trudged through scorching lands,
Through rain—and snow,
Who bartered with famine—thirst—
And death—to give me birth.

But I go on in silence,
For those who know my life
Will sing my song,
Song of the Highway,
Long, white, winding Highway.

New York, 1931

Conscription—1940

The women had few words,
They sat about mutely,
Twisting their wedding bands round and round
On their fingers, while the men talked and talked.

It was a strange new utterance, laborious speech
Of those whose tongues had been silent
While they tended the great machines—
Machines were what counted—a man's talk was nothing.

For weeks they watched the papers while Congress wrangled,
And struggled with their words.
The young men spat out their anger,
The old men chewed their nails and nodded their heads.
And when the age-clause dropped to thirty-five,
The old men chattered like monkeys.
Some told bawdy jokes about the good old days of
   'seventeen,
And some wrote letters-to-the-editor saying,
   "Dear Jim, We almost envy you today."

When it was all settled, almost everybody
   shrugged his shoulders,
They'd sign up all right—
Americans are like that—

Nobody wanted to kill anybody,
All they wanted was something to work at
And food that wasn't marked with relief stamps,
Yet nobody wanted to be called a draft-dodger.

But a few quiet boys, mostly Quakers, sat around together,
After long silences and much praying and more silences,
All night many nights,
They declared they wouldn't kill anybody—
They'd plant trees,
Or build roads,
Or stop floods,
Or give their bodies for experiments,
Or go to jail—
But they weren't going to carry a gun!

War Widow

Oh stand erect
Defiant tree!
Thrust stalwart head
Against the storm.
Grow, solitary leaf,
Burst free from root and bough
And blight and worm
To mate with wind
And keep your tryst
With history.

Woman and Man

Woman in travail
Bulging with the unborn,
Leaden with waiting,
What can man give
Worthy of your pain?
Shall he, too, feel future nations
Stirring within him,
His manhood withheld
Until he know equivalent pain,
Gushing forth in blood and tears?

Nazarene

Say that he was legend,
The dream of slaves and beggars,
Or hippy poet so charged
With music of the spheres
That stones sang beneath his naked feet.
I care not if he lived
Or uttered any word,
Or healed a single leper.
I know only that his name
Reveals that gift of pain
That only love can bear
And having borne still cry
"I love."

Death of a Friend

There was one among us who rose
And leaving by an outer door
Closed it silently.
Why have I felt a chill upon the earth
And songs of dead poets haunted me all day?

Berkeley, April 1945

Conflict

Some day the poet and warrior
Who grapple in my brain
Shall lock in final contest
And I will be ground under.
For I must sing, and yet
I wield a sword whose point
Shall find my breast when all is done.

Prophecy

I sing of a new American
Separate from all others,
Yet enlarged and diminished by all others.
I am the child of kings and serfs, freemen and slaves,
Having neither superiors nor inferiors,
Progeny of all colors, all cultures, all systems, all beliefs.
I have been enslaved, yet my spirit is unbound.
I have been cast aside, but I sparkle in the darkness.
I have been slain but live on in the rivers of history.
I seek no conquest, no wealth, no power, no revenge;
I seek only discovery
Of the illimitable heights and depths of my own being.

Cambridge, 1969

IV

NO GREENER SPRING

Without Name

Call it neither love nor spring madness,
Nor chance encounter nor quest ended.
Observe it casually as pussy willows
Or pushcart pansies on a city street.
Let this seed growing in us
Granite-strong with persistent root
Be without name, or call it the first
Warm wind that caressed your cheek
And traded unshared kisses between us.
Call it the elemental earth
Bursting the clasp of too-long winter
And trembling for the plough-blade.

Let our blood chant it
And our flesh sing anthems to its arrival,
But our lips shall be silent, uncommitted.

Tears

Three times have I known tears—
When I loved you,
When I lost you,
When you lost yourself.

Counsel

Beware of body's fire,
Take less than you desire,
Count not tomorrow's need
With this day's scattered seed.

Dinner for Three

There were three who sat and drank of wine,
On food and laughter they fed,
They talked of worlds that hurtled by,
Yet of love—not one word was said.

But love was there, ah love was there—
Brighter than candle light,
The brave, the tender and the fair
Were hosts to love that night.

Prelude to Spring

When I consider how this frozen field
Will hold within its harrowed breast
A seed which shall in time
Yield bread for hungering mouths,
I am at peace—
Earth has her need of rain,
And I of tears.

Love's More Enduring Uses

Round and round I've paced these walls of sorrow
Seeking some pitying ray of light,
This darkness presses heavily upon my mind.
Oh, I am weary of eternal night.

I would be off again, heavenbent
To catch the arrows of the sun,
Bruise my wings on tips of stars,
Ranks of snowy clouds outrun.

But love, alas, holds me captive here,
Consigned to sacrificial flame, to burn
And find no heart's surcease until
Its more enduring uses I may learn.

Icarus

Now that I have climbed
The steep battlements of the universe,
Joined in heavenly discourse
And gazed daylong upon the sun,
I am weary of the stout heart's solitude,
Bewildered by mutterings of the spheres,
I would creep once more beneath a friendly stone,
My dust contained in earth's embrace.

Of Death and Doom

If on this sphere a grim and final fate
Should hurl its planetary fire,
And stricken life an instant gained reprieve
To grasp its ultimate desire;

But you and I engulfed in terror stand
Distant as pole from pole, mute, blind,
Deaf to each; through fortune thrust apart
Or fictive creatures of the mind—

Then let the furies howl their portents well
Of death and doom to quench our present hell!

New York, January 1939

Words

We are spendthrifts with words,
We squander them,
Toss them like pennies in the air—
Arrogant words,
Angry words,
Cruel words,
Comradely words,
Shy words tiptoeing from mouth to ear.

But the slowly wrought words of love
And the thunderous words of heartbreak—
These we hoard.

Aloofness

My separate self must range from star to star,
Find its moorings in the ocean's depth
And feel no touch more binding
Than fingers of wind lifting a hair.
Yet, were you not there to greet me
I would not venture past this narrow sill.

Empty of Seed

Dusk is the dreaded hour.
Empty of seed, the sower returns
And finds no blade of candlelight
To sever darkness,
No hand to lay the cloth,
No voice to call.

Paradox

I know a tendril softly twined
About a lofty oak,
Having no power to uproot,
Can gently choke.

I know between your lips and eyes
Your liquid fire can change,
Turn granite, frosty and remote,
Immobile, strange.

O arms that touch but do not feel,
O blood that beats—no heart—
Flesh, be merely flesh this night,
From steel depart!

New York, March 1938
Revised—MacDowell Colony, April 1959

For Pan

I did not know when I had climbed the hill
Past cruel rocks and thorny underbrush
That I should find so desolate a place.
There land ended on barren cliff,
There earth and sea embraced
In perpetual union of tenderness and strife—
Unyielding stone against relentless wave.
There was the loneliness of God
Molding the first small world in mist and flame.

I would have fled the awful emptiness
Had I not seen you standing there,
Poised lightly as a gull on swirling surf—
Bright promontory of defiance—
Your arms flung windward,
Your hair a golden pennant.
And though no word was uttered
Above the tumult of advancing tide,
You came uncalled
And placed your hand in mine.

There on the furthest rim of earth
We stood, my hand in yours,
Your breath upon my cheek,
Our wild impatient dreams
Thundering echoes of the flood,
Our laughter mocking ancient shibboleths,
Shattering boundaries of space and time.

Beloved comrade, high-hearted rebel,
If I had paused,
Let wisdom shield the vulnerable heart,
I would have walked a safer path,
Crept blindly underground
And never glimpsed your shining essence,
Earth-trapped star on lonely height.

MacDowell Colony, April 1959

Anguish

Two things have sorrowed me this day—
A face like death
Where peace has come to rest
And captive love has fled;
The other, wild thing
Torn free, to seek
A sterile breast
Where dwells no memory.

A Presence

You came so softly
No shadow fell.
I heard no footstep.

Are you mortal
Or a tear behind the eyelids?
Or a sob trembling on a sleeper's lips?

New York, March 1938

Memo in Bronze

For this I love you most—
Bent to your cross
You stagger up the unending hill,
Yet turn to lift my load
And bless me with a smile
So crossed with pain,
That were my heart stilled
It would throb and beat again.

Returning Spring

I'll sink my roots far down
And drink from hidden rivers,
Renew my kinship with growing things—
The little ants will hold their congresses
Upon my arm, and cautious insects
Will make brief tours across my brows
And spiders spin webs from toe to toe.

The spears of sun will prick
No blade of grass to wakefulness
But I shall feel it tremble,
No further straw be laid upon a nest,
No twig but I shall see it quiver.

I'll hear the symphonies within a stone,
Catch every murmur of the ground,
Travel the heavens with each vagrant cloud
And mark the golden islands in the sky.

Unconquerable Dust

You are the earth
Binding me as the earth binds.
Though I may clutch at you
And hold great handfuls of you,
I am but a child pawing the desert—
I cannot contain you.
And though I stretch out my arms
I cannot encircle you.
If I fashion my heart into a rod
Thrusting its full weight thereon
I cannot reach the core of you; or climb
Through desperate loneliness to unglimpsed heights,
I cannot scale the mountain-regions
Of your dreams.

New York, February 1938

The Wanderer

I. *THE QUERY*

I come with the young sun strong in my limbs
And fresh winds in my hair;
Spring follows my footsteps,
Joy spills from my eyes,
Peace lies in my breast,
A thousand songs tremble in my brain,
My heart is merry with songs—

Will none heed young love from the hills?
No one in the loud city reveal himself?
No friend along these many streets?
Will none walk with me in the twilight?
Must love be desolate this long night?

II. *THE ANSWER*

Lonely wanderer, impatient seeker,
What if your riven heart
Screams pain to cloudbeaten heaven?
It counts little. Tonight, all night,
In this city of loneliness,
In every crack and corner,
Though tables are burdened and music bleats,
Many come hungered and longing
But go away unsatisfied.

Though thousands move together
Through clash of metallic laughter,
And though the streets swell with man-juices,
Yet each lies down alone at last
Crying after his lost desire.

III. *THE ENTREATY*

O sorrowed and despairing one,
I have listened.
I have heard you across the centuries.
When the first man stood on the edge of time
Shivering with newness, clutching at light,
Felt warmth but could not take hold of it
And ran shrieking his terror through the great spaces,
You were that cry and I the earth
That bore your footprints.

I have heard you in every sound of earth,
In the call of every sparrow and starling,
In the pleading of every whelp and cur,
In the screeching of gulls on the frozen lakes
Of the world, in the wailing of tumultuous winds
That uprooted cities and flung them into the sea,
In the bellowings from volcanoes
And in the silences of star-music.

I have heard you in the incessant chatter
Of a brook speaking with many tongues,
And when a solitary wind came sweeping
Down a vast green orchestra of trees
And set them singing as ancient violins.

I have heard you crying from prisons and madhouses,
From galleys of slaveships, in screams of the dying,
In man's elemental throat gurgles at morning,
In the whimperings of frozen puppies,
In the mewings of half-drowned kittens,
And in tremulous whispers of frightened children.

I have seen you in every beggar, every migrant waif,
In every helpless, inarticulate small thing,
In every trodden, meek, despised creature;
In the faces of doomed men pressed to cold bars,
In the silent agonies of men of great visions,
In the last lift of the finger at the deathbeat,
And in the blood and weeping of the first lifebeat.

I have felt you in the life-pulse and sweep,
In the fleet hooves of hill-deer and the waft
Of doves' wings; in the serenades of katydids
And in the wisdom of swampfrogs,
In the musings of little grey mice,
And in the preening of turkey-cocks;
In the aloofness of eagles and housecats,
In the embrace of twin snowflakes,
The tenderness of pregnant mothers,
The comrade's handclasp and the compassion
Of the Nazarene.

And I lean on the arms of night
And wait for your coming, even as I wait
For the sun to leap over cloud-fences.

Do not hesitate, my beloved,
Do not frown and turn back
When you see it is only I waiting.
If you come, feathered symphonies
Will venture on the damp twigs,
If you turn back
The squirrels will not gather nuts,
The sparrows will scorn their crumbs,
Crickets will forget their chirping—
Doves will be robbed of their cooing
And all the lizards will die under their stones.

Do not send me away, my beloved.
Come with me and we will go singing
All our days, brimming with laughter,
Touched with the sun.

New York, March 1940

Conquest

Last night you were a river
Swollen with March thaws,
Ruthlessly tearing my roots
Until, rudderless, I was borne,
A fragment in your flood.
When you are once more self-contained
In your swift channel
Shall I find reassuring earth
Beneath me and, restored,
Let dancing shadow mark your passage?

Love in Wartime

Hold me with urgency of flesh
Before a holocaust.
How the butchered dead must pity us
In whom time garnered up the worst!

If, when this awful thing is done
And I am cast upon some foreign earth
To wander senselessly among the slaughtered,
Gather up the fragments of my soul
And build it piece on piece again
Into a thing fit for God to behold,
Will you be there to watch with kindly eyes
And make a friendly place of death and ruin?

Redemption

Suffused in April twilight
I lie beside you.
Still as a sepulchre
The room is vibrant with soundless voices.
Each nerve and sinew finds its counterpart,
Clings, blends and communes
Without touch or speech.

In this moment of benediction
You have retrieved your Siegfried's blade
From years of rusted grief,
While I, bright sword redeemed,
Will flash once more in battle
To blind the eyes of tyrants.

ACKNOWLEDGMENTS

Grateful acknowledgment is made to the following publications and publishers: *Common Ground, Crisis, Opportunity, Saturday Review, South Today, Voices,* Doubleday, *The Poetry of the Negro;* Hill and Wang, *American Negro Poetry;* Wishart, *Color.*

The lines that introduce Section II are copyright 1951 by Langston Hughes. Reprinted from "Selected Poems," by Langston Hughes, by permission of Alfred A. Knopf, Inc.

ABOUT THE AUTHOR

Poet, memoirist, lawyer, activist, and Episcopal priest, Pauli Murray (1910–1985) helped transform the law of the land. Granddaughter of a slave and great-granddaughter of a slave owner, Murray was orphaned at age four, and sent from her birthplace of Baltimore to segregated Durham, North Carolina, where she was raised by her aunt. Murray left the south at age eighteen to attend Hunter College in New York City. Rejected from graduate study at the University of North Carolina because of her race, Murray worked as a labor organizer.

An early Freedom Rider, she was arrested in 1940 for sitting in the whites-only section of a Virginia bus, an event that propelled her to Howard University Law School, where she graduated in 1944, only to be rejected for postgraduate studies at Harvard Law School because of her gender. Undaunted, Murray, a self-described "opener of doors," went on to become a legal theorist and activist of lasting influence whose legal reasoning was pivotal to Thurgood Marshall's challenge to segregation in *Brown v. Board of Education*. Her idea of "Jane Crow"—that discrimination by race and by gender could be fought using the same legal argument—influenced the work of the President's Commission on the Status of Women, to which she was appointed by her friend Eleanor Roosevelt in 1962. Murray's push for an NAACP for women led Betty Friedan to found the organization that became NOW. Her work with Ruth Bader Ginsberg in the early 1970s provided the foundation of Ginsberg's argument before the Supreme Court that "equal protection" under the Fourteen Amendment encompasses not just race but gender. In 1965, Murray became the first African American to earn a doctorate of law from Yale Law School and, in 1976, the first woman to be ordained a priest by the Episcopal Church.

Murray accomplished these "firsts" while struggling with depression, chronic fatigue, financial worry, and feelings of sexual "in-betweenness." Through her life experience, legal reasoning, and spiritual searching, Pauli Murray understood that individuals have multiple identities; she used that knowledge to inspire and help fuel the twentieth century's greatest campaigns for equal rights.